D0931339

December 13, 2003

to Asha and Michael

Hold onto your dreams!

Jean Alicia Elster

I HAVE A DREAM, TOO!

JEAN ALICIA ELSTER

ILLUSTRATED BY
NICOLE TADGELL

JUDSON PRESS ▪ VALLEY FORGE

To my daughter, Elizabeth, and my son, Isaac —J. A. E.

With deep love and appreciation for my husband, Mark —N. T.

I HAVE A DREAM, TOO!

© 2002 by Judson Press, Valley Forge, PA 19482-0851
All rights reserved.

No part of this publication may be reproduced, stored in a retrieval system, or transmitted in any form or by any means, electronic, mechanical, photocopying, recording, or otherwise, without the prior permission of the copyright owner, except for brief quotations included in a review of the book.

The Scripture quotation on page 3 is from the New American Standard Version of the Bible.
Joe Joe's library book, *The Life and Works of Mary McLeod Bethune*, is a fictional creation. The information attributed to that book was gleaned from the following sources: Catherine Owens Peare, *Mary McLeod Bethune* (New York: The Vanguard Press, Inc., 1951); and Audrey Thomas McCluskey, Elaine M. Smith, eds., *Mary McLeod Bethune: Building a Better World* (Indianapolis: Indiana University Press, 1999).

Library of Congress Cataloging-in-Publication Data
Elster, Jean Alicia. I have a dream, too! / Jean Alicia Elster; [illustrated by] Nicole Tadgell.
 p. cm. – (Joe Joe in the city)
SUMMARY: As he reads about Mary McLeod Bethune, a boy learns to hold onto his dream of going to college and works to make it happen, despite the teasing of his friends. ISBN 0-8170-1397-0 (alk. paper)
[1. Perseverance (Ethics)—Fiction. 2. Self-realization—Fiction. 3. Conduct of life—Fiction. 4. Christian life—Fiction. 5. African Americans—Fiction.] I. Tadgell, Nicole, 1969-, ill. II. Title. III. Series.
PZ7.E529 Iae 2002   [Fic]—dc21   2001038917
Printed in China.

08 07 06 05 04 03 02

10 9 8 7 6 5 4 3 2 1

Then Joseph had a dream,
and ... he told it to his brothers, ...
—Genesis 37:1

Joe Joe had good news. School was out, and he wanted to get home as soon as he could. He had something important to tell his parents. He ran past the library. Then he stopped and turned around. Something was different. A worker was standing on a ladder. He was polishing a big, brass sign over the front door of the library. *Bethune Branch Public Library* was engraved in the polished brass.

"Hey," Joe Joe thought to himself as he walked back toward the library. "That sign is new!"

Since he was at the front door, Joe Joe decided to go in and tell his friend Mrs. Morgan his good news.

Mrs. Morgan was sitting behind her desk at the computer.

"Mrs. Morgan..."

She looked up with a smile. "Hello, Joe Joe. What brings you here today?"

"Mrs. Morgan, I've got some great news. Oh, nice sign out front, by the way...! But guess what?"

Mrs. Morgan stood and walked around her desk to stand in front of Joe Joe. "Tell me," she smiled.

"I got my report card today," Joe Joe almost shouted. "All A's and one B—in handwriting!"

"Why, Joseph Rawlings Jr., that's wonderful news!" She clapped her hands proudly. "Thank you for stopping by to let me know. And while you're here, I have something I've been holding for you until your next visit." She took a book from one of the piles on her desk and handed it to Joe Joe.

"*The Life and Works of Mary McLeod Bethune,*" Joe Joe read out loud. "Bethune? The person this library is named after?"

"The same Bethune," Mrs. Morgan nodded. "And I think you'll like this book about her. Take it over to the check-out desk now, and then hurry home. I know your parents will be thrilled to hear your good news."

"OK, Mrs. Morgan. Thanks!" he said, waving good-bye.

Joe Joe was out of the library and on his way home in just a few minutes, his new book tucked under his arm.

"Hey, Joe Joe!" It was Joe Joe's friend Kalia. She and Tyrone were hanging out on the stoop outside Joe Joe's house when he dashed around the corner.

"Hey, Joe Joe, what's the rush?" Tyrone asked.

"I want to show my parents my report card. Look," Joe Joe pulled the paper out of his book bag. "All A's and one B!"

Tyrone and Kalia were not impressed.

"Man," Tyrone said, "I thought you had something big happening."

Kalia giggled.

"And listen," Joe Joe ignored their grins as he put the paper away, "you know that paper we have to write for Friday? The one where we have to write about our dream for the future? Guess what I'm gonna write about!"

"How are *we* supposed to know, Joe Joe?" Kalia rolled her eyes.

"My paper's gonna be called 'Why I Want to Go to College'!"

Tyrone stepped back. "College? Come on, man. *Nobody* in this neighborhood goes to college. Who around here do you see going to college?"

Kalia just shook her head.

"My dream is to win the lottery and drive a low, fast car." Tyrone swooped his hand out close to the ground, imitating a fast-moving sports car. Then he turned to Kalia and gave her a high five. They laughed.

"Well," Joe Joe started to say, "my mom..."

But Tyrone and Kalia were already walking away.

"See you later, Joe Joe," Kalia waved without turning around.

"Sweet dreams!" Tyrone called out.

Joe Joe shrugged and climbed the steps to the front door. He went in and ran straight to the bathroom to wash his hands.

"Hi, Joe Joe," his parents called to him from the kitchen.

"Hi!" he called back.

He saw his grandmother sitting in the dining room.

"They're clean, Grandma," he said as he held out his hands.

His grandmother smiled and held out a plate of sugar cookies. Joe Joe took a couple and then remembered why he had run home.

"Hey, everybody, guess what?"

Joe Joe's mom and dad came into the dining room. "What's up, Joe Joe?" Dad asked curiously.

Joe Joe pulled the report card out of his book bag and thrust the paper at his parents.

"Look what I got on my report card! All A's and one B—in handwriting!"

His dad gave him a high five. His mother hugged him.

"Congratulations, Joe Joe! You've been working so hard in your classes," his parents said excitedly, both talking at the same time.

"This calls for a special dinner," his grandmother announced.

"You're right," his mother agreed. "And we've got something else to celebrate," she said to Joe Joe. "Your father is back to his regular shift at the factory because the afternoon welder came back to work. And I'm working days at the hospital for a while. That means we can all eat dinner together for the next few weeks!"

Grandma asked, "How about fried chicken, corn on the cob, peach cobbler..."

"And you know I want some of your famous fried-green tomatoes," Dad added with a grin.

"Green potatoes!"

Everyone turned to where Joe Joe's little brother, Brandon, was sitting in a corner playing with his truck.

"No, Brandon, *tomatoes...*" Joe Joe corrected him.

"Green *potatoes!*"

The whole family laughed.

That evening, as the family joined hands at the dinner table, it was Joe Joe's turn to say the blessing.

"Dear Lord, thank you for this food. Thank you for helping me get a good report card. And, most of all, thank you for letting us all be together for dinner today! Amen."

Then Joe Joe shared his idea for the paper he had to write about his dream for the future.

"It's gonna be called 'Why I Want to Go to College'!" he declared.

"College! That's wonderful, Joe Joe," Dad said.

"You remember that I went to the community college for two years for my nurse's license," Mom added. "It's always been *my* dream to go back and get my four-year degree."

"Maybe we can go to college together!" Joe Joe suggested, his eyes bright with excitement.

"Well, we'd better start saving up our money *right now.*" Dad winked at Joe Joe's mother.

That night, after Joe Joe climbed into bed, he opened the book on Mary McLeod Bethune.

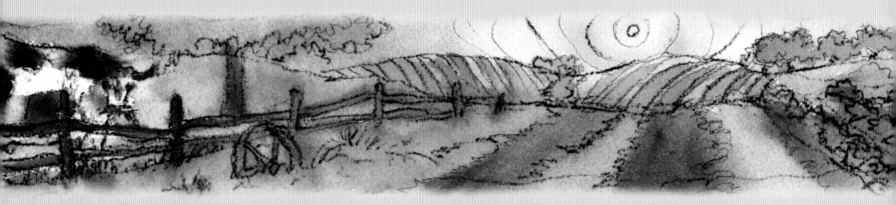

Mary Jane McLeod was born in 1875 in South Carolina. Her parents were sharecroppers; they farmed land that belonged to someone else. But Mr. and Mrs. McLeod worked hard and saved enough money to buy thirty-five acres of their own land! That was a rare thing for a black family just out of slavery.

The McLeod family owned something else—a Bible. It lay on a shelf while the family prayed and sang hymns together by the fireplace each evening. It lay there because no one in the family could read.

Joe Joe looked around his room. He saw his school books, his library books, his own Bible. What would his life be like if he could not read?

When Mary McLeod was a young girl, there were still very few schools in the South where African American children could learn to read and write.

Still, although Mary could not read, there were two things she could do: She could work as hard as anyone, and she could dream. More than that, she had faith that with hard work, her dreams would come true.

Joe Joe put down the book. He thought about his own dream of going to college. He thought about the McLeod family working and saving to buy their own land. Then, just as he drifted off to sleep, he had an idea….

The next day, right after school, Joe Joe headed around the corner from his house to Mr. Booth's store.

"Hi, Mr. Booth," Joe Joe said as he pushed open the door to the grocery store.

"Why, Joe Joe," Mr. Booth answered as he looked up from the cash register. "How have you been? I haven't see you for a while."

"I've been real busy at school," Joe Joe answered. Then he told Mr. Booth about his report card and his paper and how he wanted to start saving money to go to college.

Many African Americans in the South earned their livings like the McLeods did, although only a few owned their own land. Here a family works in a field, picking cotton.

"Mr. Booth, do you think I could work for you here at the store?"

"Well, I see a lot *has* been going on since I last saw you," Mr. Booth said as he walked around to the front of the counter. He leaned against the counter and studied Joe Joe thoughtfully. "How old are you, Joe Joe?"

"Ten," he answered.

"Well, ten years old is a little too young for me to hire you to work the register here."

"Oh." Joe Joe looked down at the floor and shifted his feet awkwardly.

"But, when my son was your age, I used to pay him a little something to help me out on Wednesdays when the delivery truck came. I could give you—"

Joe Joe didn't even hear the amount. He was too excited! "Thanks a lot, Mr. Booth. I'll see you on Wednesday after school!"

"Make sure it's OK with your parents before you come," Mr. Booth cautioned.

"I will. Thanks again!" Joe Joe said as he ran out the door.

Standing outside the store were Tyrone and Kalia.

"We wondered where you were rushing off to. You've been in such a big hurry lately," Kalia said, looking at Joe Joe.

"What's up with you and the store?" Tyrone asked.

Joe Joe told them about his plans to start saving money for college. He told them how Mr. Booth had said he could help out every Wednesday on delivery day.

"So, the college boy is working at the grocery store!" Tyrone looked over at Kalia and elbowed her. "Shouldn't he be home studying?"

"Yeah, Joe Joe. How are you going to make all A's on your next report card?" Kalia asked Joe Joe with a giggle.

"Anyway," Tyrone added, "if you really want to make some money, you could make more running for Cecil than you'll *ever* make at Old Man Booth's store. Think about *that*."

Tyrone grabbed Kalia by the arm. They both dashed away down the street.

Joe Joe *did* think about it.

"Cecil," he thought. He didn't know exactly what Cecil did, but he knew where his house was, just up the street. Joe Joe's parents had often warned him to stay away from that house. Joe Joe walked slowly home.

When he got there, he found his mother sitting at the kitchen table cutting up some carrots. She looked up at Joe Joe.

"Where have you been? You look all worn out."

Joe Joe told his mother about his visit with Mr. Booth.

"Mama, how much does it cost to go to college? Will we be able to afford it? Will you and I both be able to go? I thought you and Dad were saving so that we could all move to a bigger house...."

"Slow down, Joe Joe," Mom interrupted as she pushed aside the cutting board. She looked him straight in the eye. "I don't mind your going over to Mr. Booth's store to help him out once a week. I'm glad you think enough of your dream that you're willing to work for it."

She shrugged. "We *could* use a little more space here, but there's no hurry. We like it here. We'll never move far away from our friends and neighbors," she assured him as she stood.

"Besides," she leaned over and gave Joe Joe a kiss on the forehead, "if you keep up those grades of yours, you'll have colleges from all over the place offering you scholarships!"

She popped one of Grandma's sugar cookies in his mouth. "So, don't worry!"

"Thanks, Mom!"

Joe Joe grabbed another cookie and ran up to his room. He sat down at his desk and pulled out a notebook. But before he started to work on his paper for school, he opened his book about Mary McLeod Bethune and began to read.

Mary McLeod was nine years old when she realized that her life was different because of the color of her skin. One afternoon, while her mother was delivering some ironing to a family in town, Mary went to the backyard to play with their children. They had a playhouse filled with books and dolls. She picked up one of the books and began to turn the pages. One of the little girls ran over to her and yelled, "Put that down! You can't read!"

"That was mean," Joe Joe thought to himself. It made him remember how Kalia and Tyrone had teased him when he told them he wanted to go to college. He frowned and kept reading.

The young Mary McLeod was stunned and hurt. On her way home, she made up her mind that somehow and some way she would learn to read. It was her dream. She shared this dream with her family as they worked in the fields. She prayed about it every night before going to bed. Then, when she was ten years old, her dream came true.

"How did it happen? What did she do?" Joe Joe wondered out loud as he turned the page.

A northern church sent a teacher to start a school for African American children in the county. The teacher went to each home asking parents if they could spare one child from the farm work to go to school. Mr. and Mrs. McLeod chose their daughter Mary, who dreamed of being able to read.

Mary McLeod learned quickly. She wanted to keep on learning, but the school stopped at the eighth grade. Then good news came from her teacher. Someone had offered to send a student to a high school in North Carolina. Because she was the best student, Mary was chosen.

She had not only realized her dream to read; she was now being given a chance to go to high school!

"I'm going to pray about my dream like Mary McLeod did," Joe Joe thought to himself. "If she could go to school and learn to read, then I can go to college."

Joe Joe picked up his pen. But before he began to write his paper, he prayed, "Dear God, help my dream come true. Amen."

The next day was Wednesday. Right after school, Joe Joe dropped his book bag off at home. Then he headed over to Mr. Booth's store.

"Right on time," Mr. Booth said to Joe Joe as he came in through the door. "You can help me put these cans of vegetables on the shelf."

Joe Joe and Mr. Booth worked quickly. There were so many boxes to unload that they did not talk much. Then, Joe Joe heard loud voices outside.

"College boy! College boy!"

Joe Joe recognized the voices: Tyrone and Kalia.

"Don't let those kids bother you. You're doing fine," Mr. Booth assured him.

"College boy! College boy! College boy..."

When Joe Joe had emptied the last box, Mr. Booth handed him an envelope.

"You did good work, Joe Joe. I hope you come back next week."

"I'll be here. Thanks, Mr. Booth," he said. He left the store cautiously and looked around. He sighed in relief when he saw that Tyrone and Kalia were not waiting for him.

Joe Joe walked home slowly. He kept hearing the voices of his friends shouting over and over, "College boy, college boy..."

"What's so bad about wanting to go to college?" Joe Joe asked himself defensively.

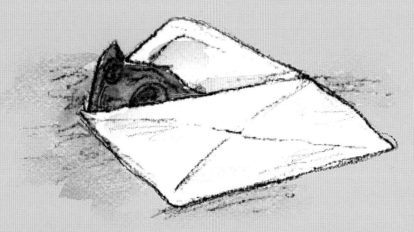

When Joe Joe got home, everyone was in the kitchen.

"How was work?" his mother asked.

"Fine," Joe Joe answered quietly.

"Did Mr. Booth pay you?" asked his father.

Joe Joe held up the envelope. "Yeah, he paid me," he answered as he headed up the stairs to his room.

Joe Joe sat at his desk. His paper was due in two days, but he did not feel like working on it. He picked up his library book. He wanted to know what happened next to Mary McLeod Bethune.

Mary McLeod wanted to use her education to help people. Back at home, she had heard someone speak at church about the many needs of people living in Africa. Because of that talk, she now had another dream. She wanted to be a missionary to Africa!

"Now, *that's* a big dream," Joe Joe grinned as he read.

When she finished high school, Mary McLeod was that much closer to her dream. Then she was accepted at a two-year college in Chicago. It was a school that would prepare her for missionary work in Africa.

As soon as she finished college, Mary wrote to a church mission group. She asked them to send her to work in Africa. She was ready to realize another dream. But instead, she received disappointing news. The mission group told her there were no openings for an African American missionary in Africa.

Joe Joe was shocked. He put a bookmark at that page and closed the book. "Dream's over," he said to himself. He did not work on his paper at all.

On Friday evening, Joe Joe's parents were talking in the living room when the telephone rang. Joe Joe was in the kitchen, helping Grandma set the table for dinner when his mother answered the phone. Joe Joe could tell by the look on Mom's face that something was wrong.

"Thanks for calling. We'll talk to him about it," his mother said.

"What's wrong?" Dad asked as Mom hung up the phone.

"That was Joe Joe's teacher. She called because Joe Joe didn't turn in his paper today. The one he was supposed to write about his dream for the future..."

"Oh, no!" Dad exclaimed.

Joe Joe bit his lip, dropped the silverware on the table, and fled upstairs.

"I'll go up and talk to him," he heard his mother say as he dashed into his room.

Mom knocked quietly on the bedroom door before entering. Joe Joe was lying on the bed with his back to her.

"Your teacher just called," she told him.

Joe Joe rolled over and looked up at the ceiling.

"Why didn't you turn in your paper?"

Joe Joe was quiet for a moment before he turned his head to look at her. "Mama, maybe I shouldn't go to college."

"Oh, Joe Joe. Don't give up on your dream!"

She went over to his desk and picked up the book about Mary McLeod Bethune.

"You know, I read some of this book when you first brought it home. Last night, I jumped ahead and started reading where you left off. A lot happened after that mission group turned Mary McLeod down. She taught at two schools for black kids in the South. She met and married her husband, Albertus Bethune. And then she realized her *biggest* dream, Joe Joe. Listen to this."

In 1904, with one dollar and fifty cents in her pocket and five students willing to learn, Mary McLeod Bethune started her own school. The students used boxes for desks and berry juice for ink—but they learned! Mary worked hard and the school grew. In three years, 250 students were enrolled! The school became Bethune-Cookman College. It expanded until it became a four-year college.

"And can you believe this, Joe Joe?" His mother continued reading.

In 1936, President Franklin Roosevelt gave Mary McLeod Bethune a special position in the National Youth Administration in Washington D.C. Never before had an African American woman held such an important job in the federal government.

"That's what can happen when you hold on to your dream!" Joe Joe's mother said to him, smiling.

"Now, your teacher said if you turn the paper in on Monday, she won't lower your grade for being late." Mom put the book down on his bed and bent down to give him a kiss.

"We love you, Joe Joe," she said as she left his room.

Joe Joe thought about his dream. He thought about Mary McLeod Bethune and her dreams. He closed his eyes and said a quick prayer. Then he rolled off the bed, went over to his desk, and took out his notebook. Sitting down, he thought for a minute and then began to write.

Mary McLeod Bethune stands with her students during a convocation ceremony in 1941.

(inset) Mary McLeod Bethune visited the White House many times in her lifetime. Here she is shown (third from the left, wearing the hat) standing behind President Harry S. Truman.

On Monday, Joe Joe was in a hurry to get home from school. He had more good news to share with his family. His teacher had asked him to read his paper in front of the whole class!

"Hey, Joe Joe—wait for us!" Tyrone and Kalia shouted breathlessly as they ran to catch up.

Kalia spoke first. "I liked your paper, Joe Joe."

Tyrone took a step back and rolled his eyes.

"I think I might want to go to college, too," she added.

"You, too, Kalia?" Tyrone asked. "I told *both* of you: No one around here goes to college—"

Joe Joe cut him off. "No, *you're wrong*, Tyrone." He looked over at his other friend. "*We're* going. Right, Kalia?"

She grinned and gave him a high five.

"Right, Joe Joe!"

Kim Crisp

887-9178